MEMOIRS
OF A MEAN SAX

poems by

Jean Fineberg

Finishing Line Press
Georgetown, Kentucky

MEMOIRS
OF A MEAN SAX

Dedicated to trumpeter and badass
Ellen Seeling
For 50 years of love and music

ACKNOWLEDGMENTS

Lucky Jefferson: Anthems of Ancestors
Quillkeepers Press: Wild Child
Montana Mouthful: Get Your Kicks on Route 66
Kerning, A Space for Words: Wild Child
Modern Poets Magazine: To My Saxophone
Workers Write!: The Jam session, The Wedding Gig, The Dive Bar, The Sub,
The Road Gig, The Big Tour
Finishing Line Press: Sonnet for an Imposter
Jerry Jazz Musician: All Music Has a Story, My Composer Brain is a
Laundromat
The Creativity Webzine: In the Shadow of Fame
Uppagus: The Rebel Flute
Scarlet Leaf Review: In the Shadow of Fame
Superpresent Magazine: Visitors
Autumn Press: Play Like a Man

GRATITUDE

Kim Addonizzio, for her expert council in nurturing my poetry habit
Eugenia Seeling, for being the daughter I never knew I wanted
Sha'ana Fineberg, for her sisterly wisdom and love

Publisher: Leah Huete de Maines
Editor: Christen Kincaid
Cover Art: Michele Friedman
Author Photo: Sandy Morris
Cover Design: Jean Fineberg

Order online: www.finishinglinepress.com
also available on amazon.com

Author inquiries and mail orders:
Finishing Line Press
PO Box 1626
Georgetown, Kentucky 40324
USA

Contents

INTRO

HOW WE MAKE MUSIC
A Fibonacci poem

Why
stay
confined
to merely
tones and semitones,
as though behind a sonic veil,
ears half open, eyes half closed, our harmonies constrained?
Imposing meaning on these shambolic times, scales and chords, earthly and otherworldly,
our muse delighted, subsumed in entropic ether,
we stitch notes into new fabric—
Our bequest to those
who have more
time left
to
live

DNA

After Jericho Brown

The obsession is genetic
My mother said "practice for 30 minutes"

But I stopped before 30 minutes
The flute didn't hear me

My mother didn't hear me
My body needed a saxophone

My true voice was a saxophone
Her true voice was her body

Her body needed to dance
Dance was in her bones

My saxophone is in my bones
The obsession is genetic

MY COMPOSER BRAIN IS A LAUNDROMAT

In my brain, notes, rests,
bass and treble clefs brazenly flirt.
Spin-dizzy time signatures
get drunk on odd meters.

Sharps flatten, unnaturals abound,
and chords get tangled in knots.
A little pink fabric softener,
and out tumbles smooth jazz.

Blacks and blues, work songs,
field hollers, gospel and hip hop
sometimes slip into the white load,
trying to pass.

The dryer's questionable intonation
collects in the lint filter.
Socks masquerade as eighth notes,
And static crackles like castanets.

I don't fold the music sheets
into standard forms.
I toss them into the air,
And they craft themselves into fresh tunes.

SONNET FOR THE IMPOSTER

Beware the fiend you fear and yet embrace—
the tiny voice that hisses in your ear.
The one so many years cannot erase—
The one which second guesses your career.

The words you write are not in fact your own.
They've all been written many times before.
Your paintings and your melodies are clones.
What makes you think your pieces will endure?

Why spend another hour, another year,
to persevere like those who met the beast?
Compelled to tell the world that you were here—
your muse invoked, Calliope unleashed.

If you know you're born to do this work,
fulfill your destiny and do not shirk.

VERSE

SLEEPING BAGS IN THE BASEMENT

New York City nurses tea and whisky in her pajamas
under ten feet of snow. Some hot dog calls a rehearsal
in his building's laundry room,
and I'm one of seventeen starry-eyed hopefuls,
eager for another no-pay networking opportunity.

I'm a walking sleeping bag in my parka.
My saxophone slides down my arm
and plummets into a fresh pillow of white.
A dude asks whether I play "that thing."
 "No," I say, "I'm just hauling it for some guy, any guy."

Slogging down Broadway, my boots catch a rhythm
as I rap my power mantra—"Do your do, Do your do."
I stuff myself into the crowded elevator,
excitement in one pocket,
trepidation in another.

The jazz raises the temperature a few degrees.
I'm the only woman, and the leader gives all the solos
to the other sax player. Grinning, I say,
"Hey man, wanna pass me a solo?"
He hands me one . . . i n . . . s l o w . . . m o t i o n.

It's a fractured blues. Jackpot!
I fly in with my funky stuff,
breeze into a bit o' bebop, and climax,
holding a ridiculously high note for an absurd amount of time,
capitalizing on the reverb
from the washing machines.

Hours later, boys bump fists and exchange cards.
Nobody asks for mine, but I crash their huddles
and bestow it upon them anyway,
tumbling into the maelstrom, boots clomping,
and rap "Do your do, Do your do."

THE REBEL FLUTE

For renowned poet and teacher Kim Addonizio

I wanted a clarinet, but my mother said
it would give me buck teeth. I wanted drums,
but who wants a power-drunk kid
flailing away to Metallica in the basement?

I got a violin, but after enduring two months
of their resident screech owl, my parents presented me
with "the perfect instrument for a girl"—
a flute.

I decapitated it and blew into the head joint,
spanking the open end, simulating turkey gobbles.
I slid my thumb in and out of its orifice,
grinning as it wailed like a police siren.

I buzzed my lips on the embouchure hole
as though it were a trumpet,
(which would have been so much cooler),
convincingly mimicking farts.

Bypassing the body, and joining the head joint
to the foot joint, I composed a 3-note ditty,
entertaining my family
with infuriating regularity.

I flapped the keys mercilessly, evoking the flutter of pigeons.
I blew cigarette smoke into the mouthpiece, and gazed,
mesmerized, as it wafted up through the holes,
imagining that I had set the flute on fire.

I twirled it like a baton. I hummed while blowing,
granting the timbre some cojones.
I tooted along with rock records,
pretending it was a flying V guitar.

In college, I took it everywhere,
like a joey in its mother's pouch.
It served as an easy social entrée,
and slowly became my voice.

Finally seduced by its inherent sweetness,
I embraced its gentle power.
Now we turn air into music,
like water into wine.

TO MY VINTAGE MARK VI SAXOPHONE

I lift you
from your velvet bed,
your heft familiar in my hands.

I stroke your brassy skin,
with its worn patina, earned
from so many choruses of the blues.

My fingers settle into
the gig-worn grooves
of your mother-of-pearl keys.

Parables of protest and gratitude
flood through the full lips
of your brilliant bell.

A Coltrane spiritual,
an Ellington tapestry,
a Ray Charles love song.

WILD CHILD

This 1970s drum set is my baby, with its champagne finish
and history of being hit by the best of them.
I never wanted babies, but I mothered my immigrant niece,
with her champagne hair and history like the drums'.

Fry an egg on that hot ride cymbal, ghost notes floating up
from the snare head. Bass drum drops bombs
(not the kind she heard explode in the old country).
Tom toms boogie, like her family running for safety.

Crack the snare like a chicken bone, high hat cymbals
swoosh, fuzzy, like her curly morning moptop.
Wizened brushes whisper old secrets, like those she revealed
when she finally let me brush her hair.

All-night Latin gigs, cross stick pops the clave rhythm,
Bedazzled women with long black hair, blood red
lipstick and strappy heels, like the shoes we wouldn't
let her wear to school, but she snuck in anyway.

Punk clubs, posturing outlier goth kids pressed against the stage,
propping each other up, sliding on the beery mosh pit floor.
Her with that black leather jacket, sewed-on spikes,
steel toe boots and 9pm curfew.

Ride that funky kick drum beater down the blues highway,
lay in with the backbeat like bad boyfriends,
court danger, recalling the time the cops arrested her
drunk in her car on the railroad tracks.

Yeah, I flirt with my ridiculously big rock kit,
twin bass drums playing catch, heads straining at the lugs.
Whomp those tubs like you're beyond pissed,
Like the times I fantasized about smacking her, but never did.

BRIDGE

GET YOUR KICKS ON ROUTE 66
For Chuck Berry, Nat King Cole and The Rolling Stones

New York, NY
Dawn smells of piss and anticipation.
Eight pumped-up rockstar wannabees,
one roadie and one so-called manager
on the lookout for the magic bus.

Lewisburg, PA
I tape photos of Jeff Beck
(a blues thing, not a sexual thing)
and Janis Joplin (maybe a sexual thing)
above my cracked leather bus seat.

Toledo, OH
Pianist falls asleep on Luna Beach,
gets a second degree sunburn,
police shove her with their boots
and chase her back to our cheap motel.

Tulsa, OK
Bus driver refuses to continue
unless he's paid RIGHT NOW.
So-called manager makes 100 calls,
Hours pass, RIGHT NOW comes.

Albuquerque, NM
Roadie makes a beeline for a rabid fan,
seduces his first groupie, disappears
and reappears grinning
after we've schlepped our own gear.

Kingman, AZ
Death metal band "Ritual" is crankin' it.
Our stoned guitarist jumps onstage,
grabs their bad boy singer, they catapult backwards,
and she breaks her leg.

Los Angeles, CA
So-called manager's check bounces,
motel rooms are bolted shut.
Party at a groupie's house lasts all night,
and band gets their kicks.

BANYU'S BLUES

Cruise ship gig, crew cabins below the disco.
Ribbons of smoke from a thousand cigarettes snake
through vents, settling like a migraine carpet.
Guitar strums and thrumming drums pummel the pipes,
rumbling like a cheetah's purr.

Bacchanalian buffets cater to passengers'
insatiable overindulgence.
Shoreside locals sell cheap trinkets
while schoolchildren in shanty towns
share scant bowls of Spanish rice.

Banyu, our steward, squeezes five prayers
and a mandatory *Thousand Hands Dance*
into his ten-hour day. I ask what makes
a successful cruise ship employee.
He says "sikap tunduk" (subservience).

The nightclub's glittering globes
hang over arched alcoves,
padded leather benches line gold-papered walls,
and flecks of fluorescent light dance on the bandstand
like drunken bridesmaids.

Our tiny dressing room is a retirement home
for wobbly once-elegant armchairs
and stained sofas with stuffing incontinence.
We are banned from the bar, but the crew
sells us smuggled "water" bottles.

Musicians grumble about their paltry pay,
three times the stewards' income. Tips from
tightfisted tourists barely keep Banyu afloat,
but this coveted job beats the work
back home in Jakarta.

We share photos of our daughters.
He won't see his new baby for another year.
We promise to meet on his next cruise.
He keeps the promise; I don't.

MY BROADWAY DEBUT

Christmas in New York.
Streets are empty,
Jews fill the Chinese restaurants
and Broadway theaters.

You can see the second act
of any Broadway show for free.
People smoke outside at intermission,
and some always leave.

Just dress snazzy, act entitled,
saunter back in with the crowd,
distract the ushers,
and scan for empty seats.

I saw the Act two of *Hair*
More than a dozen times.
I memorized every move
in the naked scene.

One Christmas, I bolted onstage
in my birthday suit.
I had the time of my life
until two stage hands yanked me off.

I put the show on my resume

CHORUS

ALL MUSIC HAS A STORY

James Brown's "I Feel Good"
makes my hips bounce like bobbleheads.
My Uber driver friend saw the *Godfather of Soul*
beat his wife in the back seat of her car.

Jubilee spiritual "Wade in the Water,"
sock cymbal serves the backbeat, soloist testifies,
drums toll deep blue, signaling escaping slaves
to hide in the river from police dogs.

Hitler's favorite opera, Wagner's
"Ride of the Valkyries,"
is banned in Israel, but welcome in
 "Apocalypse Now" and "Star Wars."

Bob Marley's "No Woman No Cry" makes me cry.
Shacks in Trenchtown, Jamaica grieve
like the ghost buildings
in my old Bronx neighborhood.

White rocker girl plays "race music,"
black erasure. Prance around, flip your
Long sweaty mane, twirl a towel
and toss it to the stoned fans.

The sillier you get, the better the show.
If you play high and fast enough
and make the right faces,
Your don't need real notes, just real passion.

THE GUERRILLA DRUMMERS

I

Her drums are gifted, borrowed, traded.
She sits on her mother's tricolor handmade rug -
red for the blood coursing through her African veins,
black for the diaspora and green for the Serengeti grasslands.
She tunes her drums to the heartbeats of her ancestors.
Her ritual caressing of the consecrated batá drum
defies taboos in her adopted home of Cuba,
where men turn their backs, and women are deemed
unsuitable for communicating with the gods.

II

Her Taiko drum is born of masculine tradition. Women
must follow the three submissions: to father, husband, and son.
Her posture, the kata, requires a wide, low stance,
hips facing the drum. She punches, kicks and blocks,
melding footwork with breath. Wearing the happi cloak
and the hachimaki headband, she embraces the four principles
—energy, movement, attitude and technique. Arms flung wide,
she defies *yamato nadeshiko*, the personification
of the idealized Japanese woman.

III

She plays for the Barundi ritual dance of the royal drum,
barefoot, balancing the heavy Karyenda on her head.
Sticks whirl and click, setting a pace for the dancers.
Animal skins are stretched on hollow tree trunks,
Symbolizing the bodies of women—breast, navel, genitals.
Organized militia wage a campaign of fear and terror,
chanting of vanquishing and raping their opponents.
Still, she plays, harkening back to an earlier time
when women were officially allowed to beat this drum.

ANTHEMS OF ANCESTORS

A seductive piano montuno, congas dive in,
cowbell pumps the clave,
and couples flood the floor.

Heartbeats sync with Latin rhythms
recalling la Patria, where anthems of ancestors
seep through stone walls.

Bongos spark memories of homemade tamboras,
fashioned from buckets and coaxed into life
by field-browned hands.

Sonorous notes from the guitarrón
propel the chugging locomotive,
while children strum miniature guitars.

Trumpets proclaim proud fanfares,
as three generations of facile fingers
fire the valves in familial tandem.

Traditional wooden flutes,
abuelos to all the instruments,
flutter with folksy filigree.

The seamless stream of salsa, cha cha,
rumba, meringue and mambo
surges through the night.

At dawn, a beguiling bolero signals time to rest.
Lovers lay weary heads on shoulders
and stumble out into the sunlight.

OUTRO—SELECTIONS FROM THE JAZZER'S PLAYBOOK

THE JAM SESSION

If you're lucky, it won't be a booze-fueled free-for-all
with blowhards playing interminable solos,
or a competition where you're snubbed for playing
too few notes, or too many notes, or running your mouth
(not on the horn), which feels like a sharp stick in the eye,
and the news travels fast. Try to not get muddled in thinking,
 "I'm hot shit" or "I'm a piece of shit."

THE WEDDING GIG

A tuxedo T-shirt doesn't cut it.
Don't flirt with the bride (or groom),
or get caught eating the shrimp.
If the bride requests Ed Sheeran's "Thinking Out Loud,"
play it, and fantasize that Marvin Gaye
didn't lose his copyright infringement suit.

THE DIVE BAR

If you're a woman, convince the bartender
that you're "in" the band, not "with" the band,
and not the singer, and claim your free beer.
When the manager says you're too loud,
turn down for one tune. Hide your tambourine,
or some shit-faced reveler will grab it
and you'll never see that puppy again.
If you're playing for the door,
make sure they don't let their friends in free.
Bring your own tip jar and empty it often.

THE SUB

If you need a sub, call someone
who doesn't play better than you,
and won't talk smack about you
or try to take your gig.
Hire a woman, even though
it will make you appear weak
and diminish your street cred.

If you are the sub, don't be a jackass.
Read incorrect sheet music
with notes small as fly shit.
Compliment the leader,
volunteer for every solo, and kill it.

.

THE ROAD GIG

Eat in truck stops, sleep in buses,
carry your shit on your back,
travel miles for short bread,
arrive beat and still look sharp.
Play hard and flap your fingers
like a wild bird. Craft a cohesive solo
and quit before you're done.
Blow your pay on fifths of booze,
and be grateful for the work.

THE BIG TOUR

Don't talk to the star, even if they flirt with you.
Play nice with the sound crew—
they're frustrated musicians who control your fate.
Back off your mic at the sound check,
so it'll be loud enough for the show.
If you hate the music, keep your mouth shut,
lest you become that malcontent who gets sent packing.
Don't get cocky and imagine you've arrived.
When this glitzy tour is over,
You'll be right back with the hoi polloi.

ENCORE

PLAY LIKE A MAN

That's a mighty big horn for a girl.
You play like a man.

I am not
delicate.
I am rough hewn.
I play like a woman.

I teach my fingers
to dream in melody
like schoolchildren,
and play dreams alive.

I propel gusts
into the sinuous brass cone,
birthing jazz from the open mouth
of the saxophone bell.

My hot breath bends air
into blues, massaging the notes
until they cry with something
understood.

Why would I exude softer thunder,
dimmer lightning,
or forge a paler path
through the ether?

I play like a woman
I play a mean sax

IN THE SHADOW OF FAME

I was a tiny star
in a shining galaxy,

Backing rock stars in arenas
where nobody knew my name.

I posed for *People Magazine*
wearing only silver paint,

I played a TV show on a rotating platform,
tripping on mescaline.

I did what I thought a star should do—
seduced groupies.

The doe-eyed teenager
with "help me" scratched on her stomach,

The barmaid
who cried in my arms all night,

The bikini girl
who slept with all the boys too.

I was stranded in Acapulco
when the promoter went broke,

Locked out of a motel
when the manager spent our money on drugs.

When the shadow of fame grew long
and the big stars imploded,

Some morphed into holograms
and started GoFundMe campaigns.

I went back
To playing local clubs.

Now I'm a big star in a tiny galaxy,
world famous in my town.

VISITORS

In my tiny apartment,
I crack open a window
so the full moon
can maneuver in and out.

Iridescent aliens with grasshopper legs
skitter in and perch at my table.
Their high-pitched chatter
punctuates the lyrics from the refrigerator.

When Bastet died, she left meows
in every room, and the aliens meow back.
When I play my music, they twist, twitch and twirl
with an amusing alien dance.

I twitch too, until dizzy drunk,
we collapse on the carpet.
Thank Goddess for these visitors.
Without them, I might go mad.

REQUEST FROM THE BANDSTAND
A Fibonacci Poem

It's
my
calling
to play tunes
fondly remembered
from your wild and free salad days.
Bring on the requests, but please don't ask for one more tune.
I'm digging being a rock star
but I gotta leave
and take my
fifty
bucks
home

A Native New Yorker with a graduate degree from Penn State University, Jean lives in the San Francisco Bay Area. Her most intuitive writing appears in hypnagogia, the magical state between wakefulness and sleep. She has served as composer-in-residence at nine art centers around the USA and is the recipient of grants and fellowships from the NEA, Chamber Music America, The Doris Duke Foundation, IntermusicSF, ASCAP, Meet the Composer and the Musicians Grant Program.

As well as working as a freelance saxophonist and flutist, Jean performs and records her original music with her octet JAZZphoria and gets her kicks playing drums with her R&B cover band, The Party Monsters.

Individual poems of hers have appeared in *Poets Magazine, Soliloquies Anthology, Vita Brevis, Dove Tails, Uppagus, Literary Yard, FLARE: The Flagler Review, Riza Press, High Shelf Press, The Fibonacci Review, The Creativity Webzine, Quillkeeprs Press, Superpresent Magazine, Lucky Jefferson, Unlost Journal, The Jewish Literary Journal, Kerning, Scarlet Leaf Review, Everyday Poems, Newtown Literary, Multiplicity Magazine, Workers Write!, Shot Glass Journal, Montana Mothful* and *As Above So Below.*

www.ingramcontent.com/pod-product-compliance
Lightning Source LLC
Chambersburg PA
CBHW022044080426
42734CB00009B/1224